Brands We Know

Crayola

By Sara Green

Bellwether Media · Minneapolis, MN

Jump into the cockpit and take flight with Pilot books. Your journey will take you on high-energy adventures as you learn about all that is wild, weird, fascinating, and fun!

This edition first published in 2016 by Bellwether Media, Inc.

No part of this publication may be reproduced in whole or in part without written permission of the publisher.
For information regarding permission, write to Bellwether Media, Inc.,
Attention: Permissions Department,
5357 Penn Avenue South, Minneapolis, MN 55419.

Library of Congress Cataloging-in-Publication Data

Green, Sara, 1964-
 Crayola / by Sara Green.
    pages cm. -- (Pilot. Brands We Know)
 Summary: "Engaging images accompany information about Crayola,
LLC. The combination of high-interest subject matter and narrative
text is intended for students in grades 3 through 7"-- Provided by
publisher.
 Audience: Ages 7-12
 Audience: Grades 3 to 7
 Includes bibliographical references and index.
 ISBN 978-1-62617-288-3 (hardcover: alk. paper)
1. Crayola (Firm)--History--Juvenile literature. 2. Crayons--History-
-Juvenile literature. 3. Artists' materials industry--United States--
History--Juvenile literature. I. Title.
 HD9791.U54C7347 2016
 338.7'617512--dc23
                        2015007871

Printed in the United States of America, North Mankato, MN.

Table of Contents

What Is Crayola?

For more than 100 years, people have counted on Crayola to inspire their imaginations. Across the globe, children and adults use Crayola products to draw, color, and paint. Today, Crayola even offers **apps** that bring drawings to life. Creating art with Crayola is easy and fun!

Crayola company **headquarters** is in Easton, Pennsylvania. The Crayola **brand** is best known for children's art products. Crayons are the most famous. The company makes about 12 million crayons a day. It also makes colored pencils, markers, paints, modeling clay, and other art tools. In addition to kids' craft supplies, Crayola makes a line of drawing tools and paints especially for adults. Crayola sells its products in more than 80 countries and in 12 different languages. It is one of the most recognized brands in the world!

By the Numbers

about
3 billion
crayons made
each year

about
465 million
markers made
each year

120
standard colors
offered today

about
600 million
colored pencils
made each year

more than
400
total crayon
colors over time

A Colorful History

In 1864, Joseph Binney started Peekskill Chemical Works in New York. The company made **charcoal** and **lamp black**. These **pigments** colored things black. Joseph's son, Edwin Binney, and his nephew, C. Harold Smith, began working with him in 1880. They took over company leadership when Joseph stepped down in 1885. Then the company name changed to Binney & Smith. It began to make red pigment for barn paint. It also made **carbon black** for car tires.

In 1900, the cousins bought a mill in Easton, Pennsylvania. There, the company expanded into school pencils and black marking crayons. The cousins also developed an interest in school chalk. At that time, school chalk was dusty. It crumbled easily and was difficult to see on blackboards. In 1902, Binney & Smith created a better school chalk. It was whiter, dustless, and less crumbly. The chalk was a hit with teachers. It earned the cousins a gold medal prize!

charcoal

red pigment

Wax Origins

Wax crayons are made with paraffin wax. This comes from coal and petroleum.

Binney & Smith was a success, but soon the cousins had another goal. They wanted to create better crayons for schools. At the time, most crayons were **brittle** and made from **toxic** ingredients. Higher-quality crayons were available, but they were expensive. Binney & Smith already made black crayons. The cousins were confident they could make kid-friendly crayons in other colors, too.

In 1903, Binney & Smith began to make crayons from melted wax. Pigment was mixed into the wax to give crayons their color. The first crayons came in eight colors. These were red, blue, yellow, green, violet, orange, black, and brown. A box of eight cost only a nickel. Now, the crayons needed a name. Edwin's wife, Alice, suggested Crayola. It came from the French words *craie* and *ola*, which mean "chalk" and "oily." Crayola crayons were easy to use, affordable, and safe. Teachers and children loved them.

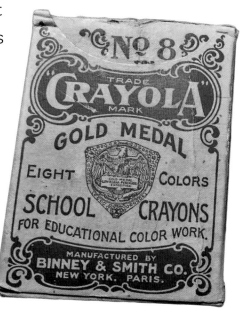

The cousins soon produced more crayon colors. Some names, such as white and rose pink, were easy to recognize. Others, such as raw **umber** and gold **ochre**, were more unusual. By 1905, the company made crayons in 30 different colors. They came in a variety of box sizes. The smallest box contained 6 crayons and the largest held all 30.

Binney & Smith continued to find new ways to package its popular crayons. In 1949, the company introduced the 48-color pack. It was the first Crayola box where crayons were arranged in **tiers**. Nine years later, Crayola introduced the 64-color pack. It included a crayon sharpener built into the box. The 64-color pack had exciting new shades, such as aquamarine, sky blue, and plum. Customers were delighted! Over time, the 64-color pack would become one of Binney & Smith's top-selling products.

They work on brains,
not batteries

1960s tagline

11

Growth and Change

In the 1950s, Binney & Smith had more than 460 different products. Crayons continued to be the top sellers. However, changing times led the company to update its crayons. In 1958, prussian blue was changed to midnight blue. Children rarely studied **Prussia** in schools anymore. Then in 1962, the color called flesh was renamed peach. This change recognized that skin comes in many shades. The company also began adding specialty colors to its collection. One new set was **fluorescent** colors. These crayons glow under special lighting!

A Misunderstood Name

In 1999, Binney & Smith changed a third crayon color name. Indian red became chestnut. People believed indian red referred to the skin color of Native Americans. However, the name actually came from a pigment commonly found in India.

Crayola factory in Easton, Pennsylvania

The company was also expanding in other ways. New factories were built to keep up with customer demand. **International** plants opened in Mexico, Canada, and England. In the United States, the company built a factory in Kansas. It also added a second factory in Pennsylvania. In 1976, the company headquarters moved to Easton to be near the main factories. The headquarters remained there even after Hallmark Cards, Inc. purchased the company in 1984.

Binney & Smith continued to add to its product line. In 1977, the company bought the **rights** to the Silly Putty brand. This stretchy, bouncy toy comes in a plastic egg. Markers were introduced in 1978. That year, craft and activity kits also became top sellers. 1987 brought colored pencils and a line of washable markers.

The company also made more changes to its crayon lineup. In 1993, Binney & Smith held a contest for customers to invent names for 16 new colors. These became part of a 96-crayon box. Winning names included shamrock, macaroni and cheese, and tickle me pink.

A World Record Holder
The world's largest Crayola crayon is located at The Crayola EXPERIENCE. It was made from small pieces of used crayons. This blue crayon weighs 1,500 pounds (680 kilograms) and is 15 feet (4.6 meters) high.

Retired Colors

Color	Year Retired
blue gray	1990
lemon yellow	1990
orange red	1990
orange yellow	1990
violet blue	1990
maize	1990
green blue	1990
raw umber	1990
thistle	2000
blizzard blue	2003
mulberry	2003
teal blue	2003
magic mint	2003

Over time, the company has **retired** 13 colors into the Crayola Hall of Fame as well. Magic mint, mulberry, blue gray, and more are no longer in boxes. Other colors, such as wild strawberry and mango tango, have taken their places. Today, Crayola crayons come in 120 standard colors. With so many choices, it is difficult to pick a favorite!

A Company Called Crayola

Over time, the Crayola name became famous around the world. In response, Binney & Smith made a big change. In 2007, it renamed itself Crayola LLC, or just Crayola. Today, Crayola's products continue to inspire creativity. Its crayons come in regular and specialty colors. The company also makes other kinds of crayons, such as fabric crayons and Twistables. Crayola's large washable crayons are perfect for young children. Crayola even offers the Ultimate Crayon Pack. It includes the standard crayons, 16 glitter crayons, and 16 "**Metallic** FX" crayons.

A Familiar Scent

A university study researched the most recognizable scents for adults. The Crayola crayon was in the top 20.

Everything Imaginable

Paint Maker

Color Alive

Jewelry Boutique

Other Crayola products are also popular. One of these is Paint Maker. It allows kids to choose and mix their own paint colors. With Jewelry **Boutique**, kids make clay beads and then design and create colorful jewelry. Color Alive combines coloring with digital technology. Kids color characters with crayons. Then they take a picture of the characters with a mobile device. A special app makes the artwork come to life!

Going Green

Crayola does more than make high-quality art products. It also helps protect the environment. The company operates a **solar** farm in Pennsylvania. The farm has more than 30,000 solar panels. These help power one of the Crayola factories. The solar panels create enough electricity to make 1 billion crayons a year. The farm also provides power to make more than 500 million markers. Today, many Crayola boxes display a sun **icon**. This means solar power was used to make the product inside the box.

solar farm

Crayola helps the environment in other ways. Many of its colored pencils are made with wood from **reforested trees**. For every tree that is cut down, one or more is planted. In a program called Crayola ColorCycle, markers are collected and recycled into clean-burning fuel. Crayola is committed to making the world a clean, safe, and colorful place for **generations** to come!

Recycled Crayons
When crayons are made, some become chipped or broken. These are remelted in the mixer to prevent waste.

Crayola Timeline

1904
The company wins
a gold medal for its
dustless chalk

1864
Joseph Binney founds
Peekskill Chemical
Works in New York

1902
Binney & Smith
develops the black
Staonal marking crayon

1880
Edwin Binney and
C. Harold Smith join
the company

1885
Edwin Binney and
C. Harold Smith take over
the company and rename
it Binney & Smith

1903
Binney & Smith
produces the first box of
eight Crayola crayons

1920
Fine art crayons
are added to the
product line

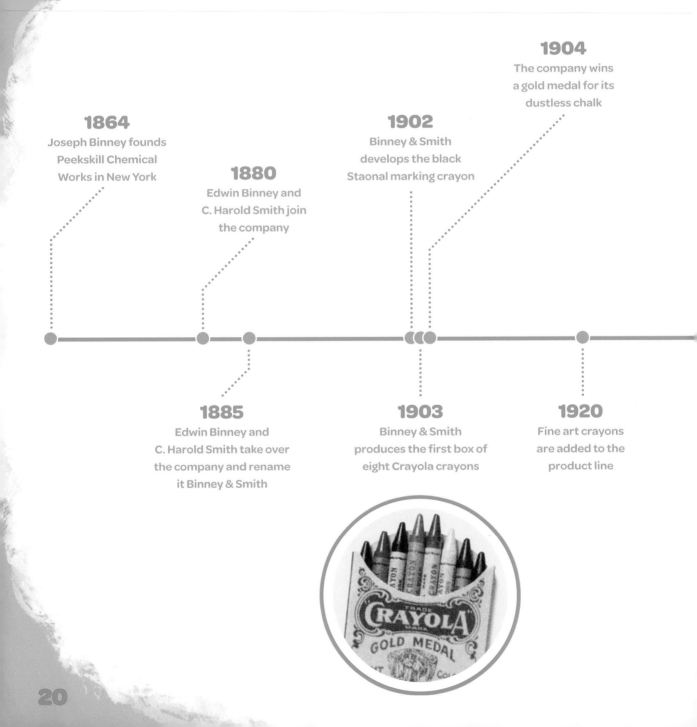

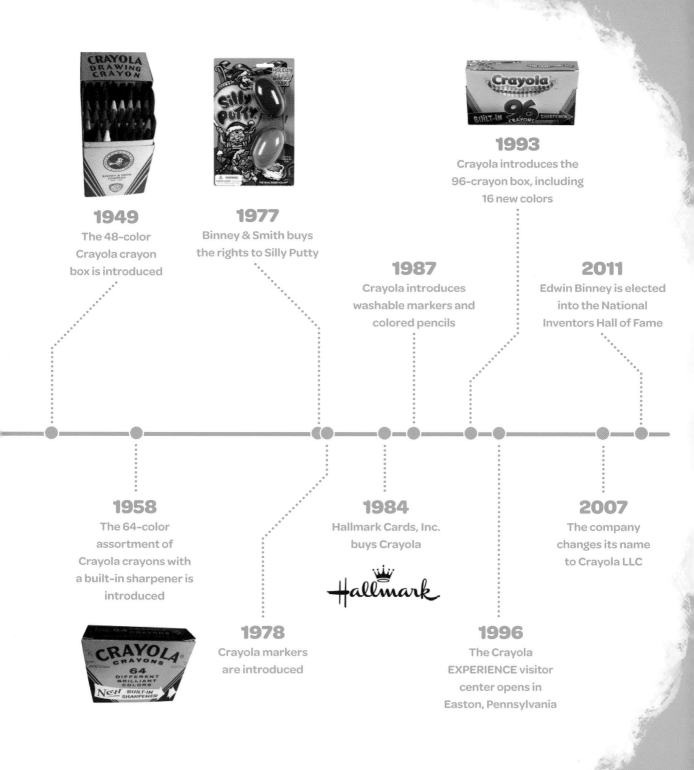

1949
The 48-color Crayola crayon box is introduced

1977
Binney & Smith buys the rights to Silly Putty

1993
Crayola introduces the 96-crayon box, including 16 new colors

1987
Crayola introduces washable markers and colored pencils

2011
Edwin Binney is elected into the National Inventors Hall of Fame

1958
The 64-color assortment of Crayola crayons with a built-in sharpener is introduced

1984
Hallmark Cards, Inc. buys Crayola

Hallmark

2007
The company changes its name to Crayola LLC

1978
Crayola markers are introduced

1996
The Crayola EXPERIENCE visitor center opens in Easton, Pennsylvania

Glossary

apps—small, specialized programs downloaded onto smartphones and other mobile devices

boutique—a small, fashionable shop

brand—a category of products all made by the same company

brittle—breaks or chips easily

carbon black—a black, sooty substance made of carbon and used in tires and as a pigment

charcoal—a hard black material made by burning wood that is used for drawing

fluorescent—very bright

generations—groups of people who are around the same age at the same time

headquarters—a company's main office

icon—a widely known symbol

international—outside of the United States

lamp black—a fine, black powder used to color things black

metallic—shiny and resembles metal

ochre—a pigment from iron; ochre can be red, yellow, or brown.

pigments—substances that give color to other materials

Prussia—a former kingdom in Germany

reforested trees—trees that have been cut down and had new trees planted in their place

retired—no longer made available

rights—the legal ability to use a certain name or product

solar—uses the sun's heat or light

tiers—different levels

toxic—poisonous

umber—a dark, yellowish brown

To Learn More

AT THE LIBRARY

Blizin Gillis, Jennifer. *Edwin Binney: The Man Who Brought Us Crayons in Many Colors*. Chicago, Ill.: Heinemann Library, 2005.

Pietromarchi, Sophie Benini. *The Color Book*. Chennai, India: Tara Pub., 2014.

Temple, Kathryn. *Art for Kids: Drawing: The Only Drawing Book You'll Ever Need to Be the Artist You've Always Wanted to Be*. New York, N.Y.: Sterling Children's Books, 2014.

ON THE WEB

Learning more about Crayola is as easy as 1, 2, 3.

1. Go to www.factsurfer.com.

2. Enter "Crayola" into the search box.

3. Click the "Surf" button and you
   will see a list of related web sites.

With factsurfer.com, finding more information is just a click away.

Index